CLASSICS *Illustrated* JUNIOR, *Paul Bunyan* Number 519 by W. B. Laughead
Cover by Dik Browne; interior art by Mike Sekowsky and Frank Giacoia; Fillers: Aesop's Fables: "The Donkey and the Little Dog" (Mike Sekowsky); "Little Boy Blue" (Alex A. Blum); "Where Go the Boats" by Robert Louis Stevenson (Alex A. Blum); (October 1955; eleven printings). From **Classics Illustrated: A Cultural History, with illustrations** © 2002 William B. Jones Jr. by permission of McFarland & Company, Inc., Box 611, Jefferson NC 28640. www.mcfarlandpub.com. New digitalized artwork: Cover by Christina Choma and interior artwork by Wayne Downey. Published by JACK LAKE PRODUCTIONS, INC. 5334 Yonge Street, Suite 902, Toronto, Ontario, Canada M2N 6V1 Copyright © 2003 First Classics, Inc. All Rights Reserved. Published with the written licensed permission of First Classics, Inc. ISBN 1-894998-02-2

PAUL BUNYAN

MANY YEARS AGO, MOST OF AMERICA WAS COVERED WITH GREAT FORESTS. AS MORE AND MORE PEOPLE SETTLED THE LAND, THESE FORESTS HAD TO BE CLEARED. THE SETTLERS NEEDED THE FOREST LAND TO LIVE ON, AND THEY NEEDED THE TREES FOR WOOD TO BUILD NEW HOMES.

THE MEN WHO CUT DOWN THE TREES FOR THE SETTLERS WERE CALLED LOGGERS. THESE LOGGERS WORKED IN LUMBER CAMPS ALL ACROSS THE COUNTRY. ALL DAY LONG THEY WORKED HARD, BUT IN THE EVENINGS, THEY LIKED TO SIT AROUND THE CAMPS AND TELL STORIES – – FUNNY STORIES AND TALL TALES. AND THEIR FAVORITE STORIES WERE ABOUT PAUL BUNYAN – – THE MIGHTIEST LOGGER THAT EVER LIVED.

PAUL BUNYAN WAS BORN IN THE STATE OF MAINE. BUT HE WAS NOT LIKE ANY OTHER BABY YOU HAVE EVER SEEN.

WHAT CAN WE DO ABOUT THIS SON OF OURS? HE HAS GROWN TWO FEET TALLER SINCE YESTERDAY!

HIS FATHER BUILT A HUGE CRADLE FOR PAUL AND ANCHORED IT OUT ON THE OCEAN SO THE WAVES WOULD ROCK THE BABY TO SLEEP.

BUT ONE DAY, PAUL STARTED BOUNCING IN HIS CRADLE . . .

. . . AND THAT STARTED HUGE WAVES THAT WASHED AWAY WHOLE TOWNS AND VILLAGES ON THE SHORE.

WHEN PAUL WAS OLDER, HIS FATHER, WHO WAS A LOGGER, TOOK HIM INTO THE WOODS TO LIVE. THERE, PAUL SPENT HIS BOYHOOD HELPING HIS FATHER CUT DOWN TREES.

ONE WINTER, THERE WAS A VERY STRANGE SNOWSTORM IN THE LOGGING CAMP WHERE PAUL LIVED.

LOOK! THE SNOW IS BLUE!

THE BLUE SNOW KEPT FALLING FOR MONTHS THE WHOLE LOGGING CAMP WAS BURIED UNDER IT.

I JUST FINISHED MEASURING THE SNOW. IT'S 200 FEET DEEP OVER IN THE VALLEY.

IT WAS SO COLD THAT WINTER, THAT EVERYONE'S WORDS FROZE JUST AS FAST AS THEY WERE SPOKEN.

I'LL HAVE TO WAIT TILL YOUR WORDS THAW OUT NEXT SPRING, PAUL, TO FIND OUT WHAT YOU SAID.

4

THE MEN LET THEIR BEARDS GROW LONG TO KEEP THEIR FACES WARM.

HEY! WATCH WHERE YOU'RE GOING! THAT'S MY BEARD YOU'RE STEPPING ON!

FINALLY THEY MADE A RULE THAT ANYONE WITH A BEARD MORE THAN SIX FEET LONG HAD TO TUCK THE END OF IT IN HIS BOOTS.

BUT IT DOESN'T LEAVE ROOM FOR MY LEGS!

ONE DAY, PAUL WAS OUT LOOKING FOR WOOD FOR HIS FIREPLACE, WHEN . . .

THAT LOOKS LIKE TWO LITTLE EARS STICKING OUT OF THE SNOW.

WHY, IT'S A BABY OX! POOR LITTLE THING, IT'S BLUE WITH COLD!

PAUL DECIDED TO KEEP THE LITTLE OX FOR A PET. HE NAMED HIM BABE.

THE FUNNY THING ABOUT BABE WAS THAT EVEN AFTER HE THAWED OUT, HIS COAT WAS BLUE.

I GUESS THAT SNOW HAS COLORED YOU BLUE FOREVER!

BABE FOLLOWED PAUL EVERYWHERE HE WENT.

BABE REMINDS ME OF WHEN YOU WERE LITTLE, PAUL. EVERY TIME I LOOK AT HIM, HE SEEMS TO HAVE GROWN A FOOT TALLER!

IN THE SPRING, PAUL BUILT A BARN FOR BABE. BUT THE NEXT MORNING...

THAT'S STRANGE. I KNOW I PUT BABE IN THE BARN HERE LAST NIGHT!

Paul's fame as a logger soon spread. Every day..

There are 50 more men waiting to join your camp.

Good. I'll come right over and build a few more bunkhouses.

In order to save space, Paul built the bunkhouses to fit on top of each other.

It's time for bed, men.

That way, Paul would stack them up at night. In the morning, he would take them down to let the men come out.

Good morning, Paul.

Paul's camp became so big that the men had to take a week's supply of food with them when they walked from one end of it to the other.

Of course, it took lots of careful planning to feed so many men. Paul and his chief cook, Sourdough Sam, talked about it for hours.

WE'LL JUST HAVE TO MAKE THE DINING ROOM TABLES LONGER.

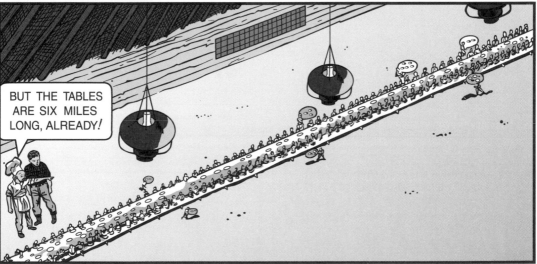

BUT THE TABLES ARE SIX MILES LONG, ALREADY!

EVEN WITH THOSE ROLLER SKATES, THE BOYS HARDLY FINISH SERVING BREAKFAST BEFORE IT'S TIME FOR LUNCH.

IT WAS SOURDOUGH SAM WHO INVENTED SOURDOUGH FLAPJACKS. THESE WERE COOKED ON A GRIDDLE TWO MILES LONG.

THE COOKHOUSE BOYS GREASED THE GRIDDLE BY SKATING BACK AND FORTH ON IT WITH BACON STRAPPED TO THEIR FEET.

OLE, THE GIANT BLACKSMITH, MADE A HUGE KETTLE FOR COOKING THE SOUP.

HERE'S THE KETTLE YOU WANTED, PAUL. IT HOLDS 1,100 GALLONS.

WHEN IT WAS TIME FOR SUPPER . . . .

THE SOUP NEEDS MORE VEGETABLES.

I'LL ROW OUT WITH ANOTHER BOATLOAD AND SHOVEL THEM IN.

IN NORTH DAKOTA, PAUL AGREED TO CUT DOWN ALL THE TREES IN JUST ONE MONTH.

I THINK I'LL HAVE TO SEND FOR THE SEVEN AXEMEN TO HELP WITH THIS JOB.

THE SEVEN AXEMEN WERE FAMOUS WOODSMEN WHO COULD CHOP DOWN TREES FASTER THAN ANYONE EXCEPT PAUL HIMSELF.

WITH THE HELP OF THE SEVEN AXEMEN, THE LOGGING WAS FINISHED IN THREE WEEKS. BUT . . .

NOW HOW AM I GOING TO GET RID OF ALL THOSE TREE STUMPS?

JOHNNY INKSLINGER, WHO HELPED PAUL FIGURE OUT HIS PROBLEMS, THOUGHT OF A PLAN.

LET'S SEND FOR SOME LARGE FIRE HOSES. I HAVE AN IDEA!

JOHNNY KNEW THAT BABE THE BLUE OX DID NOT LIKE TO GET HIS FEET WET. A FEW DAYS LATER...

THE FIRE HOSES ARE HERE, JOHNNY.

GOOD. NOW WE'LL COVER THE WHOLE COUNTRY WITH WATER.

WHEN ALL OF THE GROUND IN NORTH DAKOTA WAS COVERED WITH WATER, BABE HAD TO STEP FROM STUMP TO STUMP TO KEEP FROM WETTING HIS FEET.

HIS HEAVY WEIGHT DROVE THE STUMPS SIX FEET UNDER THE GROUND, AND THE GROUND WAS CLEARED.

AFTER THAT, PAUL HAD ANOTHER PROBLEM.

NOW THAT THE TREES ARE GONE, THE WIND FROM THE PACIFIC COAST WILL BLOW TOO HARD ACROSS THIS FARM LAND.

MAYBE WE CAN THINK OF A WAY TO PUT UP A WINDBREAK.

WE COULD BUILD A PLAIN OLD WOODEN FENCE ABOUT 200 FEET HIGH.

IT WOULD COST A LOT OF MONEY TO KEEP FIXING A FENCE LIKE THAT.

SAY, PAUL. WHAT ARE ALL THOSE HOLES IN THE GROUND DOWN THERE?

THOSE HOLES WERE MADE BY PRAIRIE DOGS AND THAT GIVES ME AN IDEA!

PAUL HURRIED BACK TO CAMP AND HAD A SPECIAL COOKSHACK BUILT WITH HOLES IN THE FLOOR.

SAM, MOVE ALL YOUR FLAPJACK BATTER AND HALF OF YOUR MEN INTO THIS NEW COOKSHACK.

NEXT, THE SPECIAL COOKSHACK WAS HITCHED UP TO BABE THE BLUE OX, AND HE PULLED IT OUT TO THE DESERTED PRAIRIE-DOG TOWN.

NOW, SAM, EVERY TIME WE STOP, YOU POUR YOUR FLAPJACK BATTER INTO THE PRAIRIE-DOG HOLES THROUGH THESE OPENINGS IN THE FLOOR.

OLE FOLLOWED, PLUGGING UP THE HOLES WITH BLOCKS OF WOOD.

PAUL KNEW THAT THE BATTER WOULD SOON START TO RISE AND IF IT HAD NO ROOM TO RISE, IT WOULD PUSH UP THE GROUND. THE NEXT DAY...

WELL, THERE SHE GOES! IN NO TIME AT ALL, WE'LL HAVE SOME MOUNTAINS HERE TO KEEP OUT THE WIND.

AND A FEW DAYS LATER..

WELL NOW, THAT'S A PRETTY NICE RANGE OF MOUNTAINS, EVEN IF I DO SAY SO MYSELF! I GUESS THAT'S AS GOOD A WINDBREAK AS ANYONE COULD ASK FOR!

THESE MOUNTAINS WERE FIRST CALLED THE SOURDOUGH MOUNTAINS, IN HONOR OF THE WAY PAUL MADE THEM. BUT LATER THE NAME WAS CHANGED, AND THEY ARE NOW CALLED THE ROCKY MOUNTAINS.

When his work was finished in North Dakota, Paul and his men decided to move further west. After a few days of walking, they came to a desert. It was very hot.

Paul became so tired from the heat that he took his ax and dragged it along the ground.

Naturally, this made a huge hole in the ground. Somebody afterward named this hole the Grand Canyon.

THERE WASN'T A TREE IN SIGHT. EVERY TIME PAUL STOPPED TO REST, 40 MEN SAT IN HIS SHADOW TO COOL OFF.

AT LAST, THE MEN BECAME SO HOT AND TIRED THAT THEY COULDN'T WALK ANOTHER STEP.

YOU STAY HERE AND REST, MEN. I'LL GO ON WITH BABE AND SEE WHAT LIES AHEAD.

THAT NIGHT, PAUL CAME TO A FARM.

I NEED FOOD AND WATER FOR MY MEN. DO YOU HAVE ANYTHING TO SELL ME, FARMER?

I HAVEN'T ANY WATER, BUT YOU CAN BUY ALL THE CORN YOU WANT.

FINE. I'LL TAKE ALL THE CORN YOU HAVE.

Paul loaded the bags of corn on Babe's back and started back to his men.

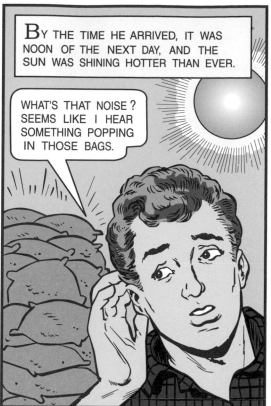

By the time he arrived, it was noon of the next day, and the sun was shining hotter than ever.

WHAT'S THAT NOISE? SEEMS LIKE I HEAR SOMETHING POPPING IN THOSE BAGS.

The sun had made the corn so hot that it was popping. Soon the air was filled with popcorn. The men thought it was snow.

SNOW! SNOW! LOOK, IT'S SNOWING! WE'RE SAVED!

AFTER A FEW DAYS OF WALKING, THEY CAME TO A VALLEY.

THIS LOOKS LIKE A GOOD PLACE FOR US TO STOP A WHILE AND GROW SOME VEGETABLES.

I DON'T KNOW ABOUT THAT. THE SOIL LOOKS GOOD, BUT THERE DOESN'T SEEM TO BE ANY WATER AROUND HERE.

BUT PAUL THOUGHT THERE WAS WATER. SO HE TOOK HIS AX AND . . .

THE SPOUT OF WATER THAT HE STARTED CAN STILL BE SEEN IN YELLOWSTONE NATIONAL PARK. IT IS CALLED "OLD FAITHFUL."

NOT LONG AFTER THAT, THE MEN ARRIVED AT THEIR NEW CAMP. ONE DAY, CHRIS CROSSHAUL CAME INTO PAUL'S OFFICE.

I BROUGHT YOU SOMETHING, PAUL.

WHAT IS IT?

IT'S A DOG. A HUNTING DOG.

I LOVE TO GO HUNTING, BUT I'VE NEVER BEEN ABLE TO FIND A HUNTING DOG THAT COULD KEEP UP WITH ME.

PAUL NOTICED THAT THE DOG'S FRONT LEGS WERE MUCH SHORTER THAN HIS BACK LEGS.

THIS DOG IS DIFFERENT FROM ALL OTHERS I'VE SEEN. MAYBE I CAN USE HIM.

PAUL HURRIED TO THE COOKHOUSE.

SAM, I NEED SOME OF THOSE FAMOUS SOURDOUGH FLAPJACKS OF YOURS.

WHAT ARE YOU USING THEM FOR THIS TIME, PAUL?

IT'S A SECRET, SAM. YOU'LL HAVE TO WAIT AND SEE.

PAUL TOOK SKOOKUM, THE NEW DOG, AND THE SOURDOUGH FLAPJACKS TO HIS OFFICE.

HERE YOU ARE, SKOOKUM. GO TO IT, BOY!

FOR WEEKS, PAUL STUFFED SKOOKUM WITH SOURDOUGH FLAPJACKS, DAY AND NIGHT. WHEN THE SOURDOUGH BEGAN TO RISE, SKOOKUM STARTED RISING ALSO. HE ROSE . . .

23

. . . AND HE ROSE . . .

. . . AND HE ROSE! AT THE END OF TWO MONTHS . . . . .

PAUL NEVER HAD TO WORRY ABOUT A HUNTING DOG AGAIN. SKOOKUM NEVER GOT TIRED, NO MATTER HOW FAR HE RAN, BECAUSE HE WAS ALWAYS RUNNING DOWNHILL!

ABOUT THIS TIME, PAUL GOT A LETTER ASKING HIM TO COME AND DO SOME LOGGING IN NEVADA. SO HE HITCHED BABE TO THE PIECE OF LAND THAT THE CAMP WAS ON AND MOVED THE WHOLE CAMP.

AS SOON AS PAUL TOOK A LOOK AT THE TREES IN NEVADA, HE GOT WORRIED.

LOOK AT THOSE THORNS, OLE! THEY MUST BE 70 FEET HIGH!

THOSE THORNS WILL KEEP THE TREES FROM FALLING DOWN, EVEN AFTER THEY'VE BEEN CUT.

BUT PAUL, AS ALWAYS, THOUGHT OF A WAY TO SOLVE THE PROBLEM.

I KNOW! WE'LL BLAST THE TREES OUT WITH DYNAMITE -- AND THE THORNS AT THE SAME TIME!

AND SO, A FEW DAYS LATER...

BOOM!

26

BUT THE NEXT MORNING . . .

WAIT TILL PAUL SEES THIS!

WELL, LOOK AT THAT!

THE TREES HAVE LANDED BACK IN THEIR HOLES, RIGHT SIDE UP!

PAUL WAS PRETTY UPSET ABOUT THIS AT FIRST. BUT SOON HE THOUGHT OF ANOTHER PLAN.

THE ONLY WAY TO GET THOSE TREES OFF THE LAND IS TO DRIVE THEM UNDERGROUND.

SO FOR 39 WEEKS, THE MEN WERE BUSY BUILDING THE BIGGEST PILE DRIVER EVER MADE.

WHEN IT WAS FINISHED, IT WAS SO TALL THAT THE CLOUDS GOING BY KEPT KNOCKING OFF THE TOP OF IT.

FINALLY, PAUL PUT IN A HINGE SO HE COULD LET DOWN THE TOP WHENEVER HE SAW A CLOUD COMING.

When everything was ready, Paul put the pile driver in place.

Babe then pulled a weight to the top of it.

The weight drove the tree 14 feet below the ground, and the crash was heard 88 miles away.

After that, the trees were driven underground at a rate of one every three minutes. In just nine days, Nevada was as bare as any desert you ever saw.

WELL, YOU CAN SEE THAT IT DIDN'T TAKE PAUL LONG TO CLEAR OFF ANY PIECE OF LAND, ONE WAY OR ANOTHER, ONCE HE SET HIS MIND TO IT.

WITHIN A FEW YEARS, PAUL BUNYAN HAD TAKEN CARE OF ALL THE BIG LOGGING JOBS THAT HAD TO BE DONE IN THIS COUNTRY.

SO HE TOOK HIS HUNTING DOG, SKOOKUM, AND BABE THE BLUE OX AND WENT OFF INTO THE MOUNTAINS TO SPEND THE REST OF HIS LIFE JUST HAVING FUN.

THE END

AESOP'S FABLES
THE DONKEY AND THE LITTLE DOG

A MAN ONCE HAD A DONKEY THAT HE TREATED VERY WELL. BUT THE DONKEY WAS NEVER SATISFIED.

I WISH I DIDN'T HAVE TO WORK SO HARD.

WHILE I TOIL IN THE FIELDS ALL DAY, YOU DO NOTHING BUT SIT IN THE MASTER'S LAP.

YOU SHOULD BE HAPPY THAT THE MASTER TREATS YOU SO KINDLY. STOP COMPLAINING.

JUST THEN, THE MASTER CAME INTO THE STABLE.

HE SAT DOWN TO LET THE DOG JUMP ONTO HIS LAP.

IT MADE THE DONKEY ANGRY TO SEE THE DOG DO THINGS THAT HE HAD NEVER BEEN ALLOWED TO DO. SO...

THE DONKEY TRIED TO JUMP ON THE MASTER AND LICK HIS HANDS AS THE DOG HAD DONE.

HELP! HELP! THIS DONKEY WILL CRUSH ME!

SO A SERVANT CAME RUNNING TO DRIVE THE DONKEY OFF.

IT IS BETTER TO BE SATISFIED WITH WHAT YOU ARE, THAN TO MAKE A FOOL OF YOURSELF BY TRYING TO BE WHAT YOU ARE NOT

THE END

LITTLE BOY BLUE

Little Boy Blue, come blow your horn!

The sheep's in the meadow, the cow's in the corn.

Where's the boy that looks after the sheep?

He's under the haycock, fast asleep.

Will you wake him? No, not I;

For if I do, he'll be sure to cry.

WHERE GO THE BOATS?

Dark brown is the river,
  Golden is the sand.
It flows along forever,
  With trees on either hand

  Green leaves a- floating,
    Castles of the foam,
  Boats of mine a-boating—
    Where will all come home?

  On goes the river
    And out past the milk,
  Away down the valley,
    Away down the hill

    Away down the river,
      A hundred miles or more,
    Other little children
      Shall bring my boats ashore.

From *A Child's Garden of Verses*
By Robert Louis Stevenson